URBAN GARDENING AND FARMING FOR TEENS™

COMPOSTING
TURN FOOD WASTE INTO RICH SOIL

BRIAN HANSON-HARDING

PUBLISHING®

New York

To Alexandra, my partner in composting

Published in 2014 by The Rosen Publishing Group, Inc.
29 East 21st Street, New York, NY 10010

First Edition

Library of Congress Cataloging-in-Publication Data

Hanson-Harding, Brian.
Composting: turn food waste into rich soil/Brian Hanson-Harding.—1st ed.
    p. cm.—(Urban gardening and farming for teens)
ISBN 978-1-4777-1781-3 (library binding)
1. Compost. I. Title. II. Series: Urban gardening and farming for teens.
TD796.5.H36 2014
631.8'75—dc23

                      2013019267

Manufactured in the United States of America

CPSIA Compliance Information: Batch #W14YA: For further information, contact Rosen Publishing, New York, New York, at 1-800-237-9932.

Contents

Introduction

If you are planning on trashing your pizza crusts and apple core in the cafeteria of Woodcreek High School in Roseville, California, you'll have to get past senior Ricky Jones first. Jones and other members of the nature center at Woodcreek High are on a mission to make sure that students don't throw food scraps into the trash but put them in the blue recycling cans designated for organic waste. After lunch, Jones and his crew place the waste in one of two huge wooden worm bins that they made, where over ten thousand worms munch on the food that students throw out. When the worms are done, they produce rich, dark, crumbly compost, which is then used in gardens and plantings around the campus. "This is something that's simple to do but that makes a big impact if a lot of people do it," Jones told Rosen Publishing. "And I like playing with the worms."

Jones and his friends have figured out how to compost the thousands of pounds (kilograms) of food scraps wasted by their school every year, and they are not alone. They are part of a growing trend sweeping the country to remove organic matter from the waste stream and put it to good use.

Composting—the breaking down of food scraps and yard trimmings into simpler compounds through the use of macroorganisms (like worms) and microorganisms (like bacteria)—has become increasingly common in recent decades. It is an essential part of organic gardening, and more and more, it is seen as a responsible way to deal with organic waste. Individuals are doing

All around the country, schools are starting composting programs that require students to separate organic waste from trash and recyclables.

it in their backyards, businesses are paying for it, and cities are requiring it. All this composting is starting to make a difference. It is improving garden soil and keeping waste out of landfills, where it would release methane—a harmful greenhouse gas— into the atmosphere.

CHAPTER ONE

WHAT'S THE DIRT ON COMPOSTING?

People have been composting since ancient times. Even the Bible mentions the use of rotted manure straw. Chinese farmers have been doing it in their rice paddies for centuries. In the United States, prominent farmers like George Washington and Thomas Jefferson promoted the use of compost. Famed naturalist Charles Darwin wrote about it in his last book, *The Formation of Vegetable Mould Through the Action of Worms*.

But in the mid-nineteenth century, scientists identified individual chemicals that promoted plant growth. "Scientific farming" took off in the early twentieth century, and farmers and gardeners began using chemical fertilizers on their crops.

Then, in the 1940s, advocates of organic gardening techniques began to champion the use of compost to improve soil quality. Since then, a growing number of American farmers and gardeners have begun using compost on their soil. While chemical fertilizers can make plants grow faster and more vigorously, their use can lead to soil exhaustion. It can also lead to chemical runoff, or the flow of chemicals into streams, rivers, lakes, and oceans with rainwater. Most chemical fertilizers consist of nitrogen, phosphorus, and potassium, each of which promotes a specific outcome in plant growth. Compost, on the other hand, has a full range of nutrients and microorganisms that will improve the soil for years to come.

BENEFITS OF COMPOSTING

These days, people compost for a number of practical, environmental, and philosophical reasons. First, compost is good for the land because it encourages the growth of bacteria, fungi, worms, and other organisms that nourish the soil. Compost can suppress plant diseases and pests, improve soil structure, reduce runoff and erosion, eliminate volatile organic compounds (VOCs) from runoff, and reduce the need for watering. It can also help stabilize the pH level of the soil.

Composting removes organic refuse from the waste stream, allowing it to decompose naturally rather than take up space in landfills. In landfills, organic waste is buried and cut off from air, and it produces methane, a harmful greenhouse gas. According to the U.S. Composting Council, 34 percent of all methane emissions come from landfills, and most of that is from food waste. Composting food waste can also save money by cutting down on the cost of trucking waste to landfills. And the more compost we use as fertilizer, the less we need to spend on producing chemical fertilizers (largely made of petroleum products) and trucking them over long distances. Finally, composting is natural: it is nature's way of using death to create new life. Nature doesn't waste anything; waste is a human concept.

At a compost farm, tree fruit, wood chips, and horse manure are turned into organic fertilizer.

According to the Environmental Protection Agency (EPA), in 2010, the United States generated about 250 million tons (227 million tonnes) of municipal solid waste, or nearly 4.5 pounds (2 kg) per person per day. About two-thirds of the nation's waste consists of organic materials—food waste, yard trimmings, and wood and paper products—all of which potentially could be composted. According to the U.S. Composting Council, in 1990, the United States diverted only 2 percent of the total solid waste stream by composting. But, as of 2006, Americans were recovering 20 percent through composting, including 62 percent of all yard trimmings. The number of large-scale food composting projects—run by municipalities, colleges, or farms—nearly

MICROBES TO THE RESCUE!

The organic material in compost decomposes as microorganisms eat it, but plastic just sits in a landfill for a thousand years before breaking down, right? That's what most scientists thought until Canadian high school student Daniel Burd did his science fair project a few years ago. According to a Reuters article published in the *Christian Science Monitor*, Burd experimented until he found the bacteria that would eat plastic the fastest. He took landfill dirt, water, two strains of bacteria, yeast, and plastic and mixed it all together. Within six weeks, the plastic had degraded by 43 percent. Burd predicts that plastic bags should be able to completely decompose within three months. That's great news for a planet that produces more than five hundred billion plastic bags a year and in which Texas-sized patches of discarded plastic float in the Pacific Ocean.

doubled between 2000 and 2007, increasing from 138 to 267, according to the *New York Times*.

Over the last thirty years, a commercial composting industry has developed. Today, the U.S. Composting Council estimates there are between four thousand and five thousand facilities producing and selling compost. But this compost is usually made from only one source, such as cow manure. Homemade, backyard compost is actually better: it requires no fossil fuels and creates no emissions. It is better for the soil because its feedstock, or raw material, comes from a variety of sources, and it is more thoroughly broken down by bacteria and fungi.

A growing number of people are composting at home. The first step is to separate kitchen scraps from other garbage.

A GROWING TREND

More and more people are composting at home, at work, and beyond. People compost kitchen scraps, grass clippings, and dead leaves in their backyards, in open piles, in homemade compost bins, or in manufactured closed composters. Others engage in vermicomposting, or composting with worms, right inside their homes. Increasingly, city dwellers bring their food scraps to compost sites in community gardens. In New York, residents can drop off their organic waste at greenmarkets across the city.

A high school student scoops compost into 40-pound (18 kg) bags that will be sold to gardeners.

All over the country, schools are starting composting programs, sometimes using the finished product on their gardens. A recycling and composting program in Portland, Maine, helped city schools reduce their trash by 50 to 80 percent, BioCycle.net reported. Launched in fall 2011, the program saved the school district $20,000 in its first year. Some workplaces are beginning to offer composting right in the office. Growing City, an organics recycling company in Vancouver, British Columbia, picks up organic waste from businesses and composts it.

In the United States, a growing number of cities are instituting mandatory composting programs, including Seattle,

Washington; Portland, Oregon; and Boulder, Colorado. According to EMagazine.com, San Francisco began mandatory composting in 2009 and now diverts 80 percent of its waste from landfills, shipping 650 tons (590 tonnes) of compostable material daily to a private composting facility. The city's goal is zero waste by 2020. In the not-too-distant future, bright green barrels full of food waste waiting to be picked up on city curbsides may be as common as blue barrels of recyclables are today.

CHAPTER TWO

BREAKING IT DOWN

Lots of people have recipes and theories for making the best compost, but it is important to remember that the process of composting is natural. As many have put it, "Compost happens." Whether you do something about it or not, organic materials will break down and ultimately become humus, the dark, rich layer of broken-down organic substances that can be found, for example, on the forest floor. Leaves, grasses, twigs, fruit, dead animals—they all become compost sooner or later. If you just threw all your cut grass, trimmed branches, pulled weeds, and discarded kitchen scraps into a pile in your backyard, they would eventually break down on their own.

But when most people talk about composting, they mean the biological decomposition of organic matter under *controlled* conditions so that the material breaks down speedily and produces a useful enhancement for garden soil. To understand how to accomplish that, we need to understand the science of composting, which breaks down into two categories: aerobic and anaerobic. Most composting systems are aerobic, which means they require the presence of oxygen. However, it is also possible to have an anaerobic system, which involves relatively little oxygen.

COMPOST BIOLOGY

Compost is a living substance, chock full of micro- and macro-organisms. By some estimates, there are more organisms in a teaspoon of compost than there are people on Earth! It is these very organisms that cause the chemical and physical changes we've been discussing. Various microorganisms—bacteria, actinomycetes, fungi, protozoa, and rotifers—all play different roles in the process of decomposition.

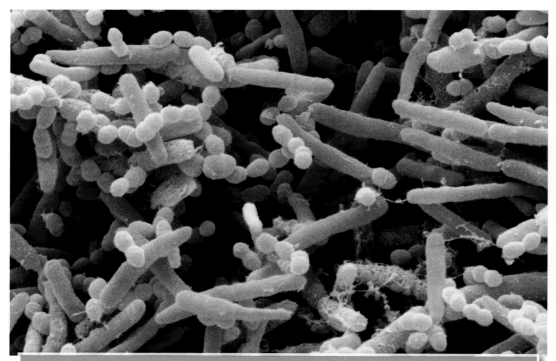

Bacteria make up 90 percent of the microorganisms found in compost. They are responsible for most of the decomposition of organic matter that occurs in the process of making compost.

Bacteria are the smallest and most numerous microorganisms in compost. They comprise up to 90 percent of the microorganisms present in compost. They're responsible for most of the decomposition and heat generation. Three basic types of bacteria dominate in compost at different times: psychrophilic, mesophilic, and thermophilic. Psychrophilic bacteria can decompose organic material even when the temperature is below freezing, but they work best at around 55° Fahrenheit (13° Celsius). In the process, they give off heat, which can make conditions right for the next type of bacteria, mesophilic. Mesophilic bacteria can survive in temperatures as low as 40° F (4.4° C) and as high as 110° F (43.3° C), but they do best between 70° F (21.1° C) and 90° F (32.2° C). If conditions are right, they can produce enough heat to activate thermophilic (heat-loving) bacteria, which thrive between 104° F (40° C) and 160° F (71.1° C). The heat they produce promotes the growth of more thermophilic bacteria, which continues the breakdown of organic material as long as enough oxygen is present. Once the compost cools down, mesophilic bacteria predominate once again.

Actinomycetes resemble fungi but are actually bacteria. They help degrade tough debris such as bark, newspaper, and woody stems and give compost its characteristic fresh, earthy smell. Some are present in the thermophilic phase and others in the final curing phase, when the toughest compounds remain to be broken down. They form long, weblike filaments that can be seen as a kind of white fuzz around the edges of the pile.

Fungi, which include molds and yeasts, also help break down cellulose (woody fibers) and other tough debris, which can then be further decomposed by bacteria. Like actinomycetes, they spread in thin filaments and live mostly in the outer layer of the compost pile. In the droplets of water within compost live protozoa and rotifers, microscopic organisms that feed on organic matter as well as bacteria and fungi.

An entire ecosystem of macroorganisms thrives in compost, including nematodes, mites, snails, slugs, redworms, millipedes, sowbugs, whiteworms, springtails, beetles, ants, and centipedes. As these invertebrates feed on organic matter, microorganisms, and each other, they help decompose the organic residues, making them available for fungi, bacteria, and actinomycetes to work on. Not only do they break down organic materials, but they also bring in air by tunneling through the pile, and they leave rich

This wood louse and millipede are two of the macroorganisms that not only break down organic materials, but also bring air into the compost by tunneling through the pile.

organic excrement in their wake. All this life is what makes compost such a rich medium in which to grow plants.

COMPOST CHEMISTRY

Carbon and nitrogen are the two main chemical elements in compost. Carbon makes up about one-half of the total mass of organisms in compost, and it's an energy source for them.

Nitrogen is usually just a small percent of the total mass, but it is essential for growth of the populations of microbes that break down organic material. Nitrogen is a crucial component of protein, and it is essential for bacteria, whose biomass is over 50 percent protein. With too little protein, the microbial population will not grow quickly enough, slowing down the composting process. Too much nitrogen can speed up microbial growth so much that oxygen gets used up. This can lead to anaerobic conditions, which cause foul smells. In addition, some of the excess nitrogen is given off as foul-smelling ammonia gas.

Savvy composters are mindful of the carbon-nitrogen, or C:N, ratio. When adding materials to compost, one should aim for a C:N ratio of about 30:1. In general, materials that are green and moist are relatively high in nitrogen: coffee grounds have a C:N ratio of 14:1; food waste, 15:1; and grass clippings, 15:1. Materials that are brown and dry are high in carbon: the C:N ratio of dry leaves is 47:1; cardboard, 378:1; and shredded newspaper, 54:1. As the materials break down, some carbon is consumed by microorganisms and more carbon is released in the form of carbon dioxide gas. The proportion of carbon decreases, as does the C:N ratio. Finished compost ideally has a C:N ratio of between 10:1 and 15:1.

ENERGY FROM COMPOST

In the 1970s, Jean Pain of France figured out a way to generate all of his energy needs from compost. His huge compost pile was about 10 feet (3 meters) high and 20 feet (6 m) across, and it generated heat aerobically to heat up the water in about 600 feet (183 m) of flexible pipe buried in the mound. Pain used this to provide all of his family's heat and hot water needs.

Pain also had a large steel tank that was three-quarters full of compost that had been soaked for two months. This wet compost decomposed anaerobically and produced methane gas that left the tank through a tube and collected in empty truck tire inner tubes. He used the methane for cooking and for running a generator that produced electricity to light his home.

HEATING THINGS UP WITH OXYGEN

Oxygen is an essential element for aerobic composting systems. Aerobic composting can occur in open piles, ventilated compost holding units, or compost tumblers. In an aerobic system, microorganisms oxidize carbon for energy. In doing so they use up the oxygen and produce carbon dioxide. As the carbon is used up, the compost condenses and the oxygen available to the microorganisms decreases. At this point, the compost needs to be aerated to continue the aerobic process. Aerobic microbes can survive in oxygen concentrations as low as 5 percent, but levels over 10 percent are best. Aerobic bacteria work hard and fast, and in the process they give off phosphorus, nitrogen,

Steam rises from an industrial compost pile during the process of aeration. Proper aeration of compost prevents unpleasant odors.

magnesium, and other valuable nutrients for plants. When done correctly, aerobic composting emits no unpleasant smells.

Below a 5-percent oxygen concentration, the process becomes anaerobic and produces unpleasant odors. These include the "rotten egg" smell of hydrogen sulfide gas and the putrid smell of the nitrogen compounds putrescine and cadaverine. Anaerobic composting doesn't generate heat and is slower than aerobic composting, but it requires much less work.

COMPOST PHYSICS

The rate at which compost breaks down depends on a number of factors, including particle size, moisture content, temperature, and the size and shape of the system. Heat is a big factor. If managed correctly, aerobic compost can reach temperatures of 100° F (38° C) to 160° F (71° C), killing weed seeds, fly larvae, and pathogens. It can get so hot that an iron bar thrust into the center would be too hot to hold.

A properly managed aerobic compost system has three phases. First, the mesophilic phase, or moderate temperature phase, lasts a few days. Next, the thermophilic phase lasts from a few days to a few months and breaks down the material. In outdoor compost systems, worms and insects survive this stage by moving off to the edges or going dormant. However, temperatures over 140° F (60° C) can destroy helpful microorganisms, so managers of industrial compost systems turn or aerate their piles to keep the temperature down. Often, turning the pile introduces more oxygen to the organic matter, so the temperature rises again. After a while, when the temperature drops and doesn't rise again after mixing, the thermophilic phase is over. This is the cooling and maturation phase, when the compost cures. The compost is now ready to use!

Just as heat is generated by the microorganisms, it is lost through conduction, convection, and radiation. Through conduction, energy is transferred from atom to atom by direct contact, from the center of the pile to the air at the edges. Through convection, heat moves through the water in the compost, rising to the top. The steamy water vapor that rises from hot compost is the result of convection. Radiation refers to the heat that radiates out into the surrounding air.

Bigger compost systems generate and retain more heat because there is less surface area in proportion to the overall volume. Generally, a compost system should be at least 3 feet (91 centimeters) high, 3 feet (91 cm) wide, and 3 feet (91 cm) deep in order to generate and retain heat.

Several other factors affect compost temperature. Moisture is key: drier composts heat up and cool off more quickly. The optimal moisture content is about 50 to 60 percent. Too little moisture—under 30 percent—leads to sluggish bacterial activity, while too much moisture—over 65 percent—leads to slow or anaerobic decomposition. In terms of particle size, smaller particles can lead to hotter temperatures because there is more surface area for the microbes to act upon. But if particles are too small and compact, there will be less oxygen available, decreasing microbial activity. Smaller particles result in smaller pores, tiny spaces in the compost that hold oxygen.

CHAPTER THREE

TURNING GARBAGE INTO GARDEN GOLD

Most people compost yard trimmings and kitchen scraps, but there is a huge variety of waste that can be composted. The greater the variety of materials, the better the compost. To make it simple, anything that has ever lived can be composted. Of course, there are practical considerations: you don't want the pile to smell, and you don't want to attract animals. Depending on the conditions of your pile and how much work you want to do, there are some organic items that are better left out.

GETTING THE RECIPE RIGHT

Materials for your compost pile pretty much fit into two categories: green (material that is rich in nitrogen and has a relatively low C:N ratio) and brown (material that is high in carbon and has a high C:N ratio). These materials are not literally green and brown, however. That's just a shorthand that gardeners use.

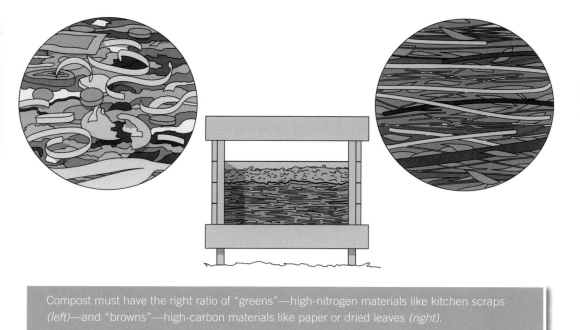

Compost must have the right ratio of "greens"—high-nitrogen materials like kitchen scraps *(left)*—and "browns"—high-carbon materials like paper or dried leaves *(right)*.

Typical "greens" include grass clippings, kitchen scraps, green leaves, tea bags, coffee grounds, herbivore manure (rabbit is best), houseplants, weeds without seeds, plant prunings, and old bouquets. You can also include some unusual items, such as kelp or seaweed, algae, and human and animal hair. People often forget about compostable liquids, such as aquarium water, cooking water, and dregs of coffee, tea, wine, or beer.

Typical "browns" include dried leaves, sawdust, shredded paper, shredded cardboard, straw, cornstalks, aged hay, and chipped wood. You can also include paper towels and napkins, toilet paper rolls, dryer lint, wood ash, vacuum cleaner dust, egg cartons, the contents of your gutters, some wrapping paper, and worn-out 100 percent cotton, wool, or silk clothing.

What should you *not* compost? Anything that will be bad for your garden, including coal ash (it contains harmful iron and sulfur), human or carnivore manure (it's a health risk), heavily coated paper (it could have unwanted chemicals), or anything treated with pesticides or herbicides. It's also a good idea to avoid diseased plants (unless you have a really hot pile), evergreen leaves (they break down *very* slowly), and walnuts (they contain a compound that inhibits the growth of some plants).

Most composting manuals advise against including meat, dairy, and grease, since they can attract unwanted pests and create bad odors. But if your pile is large enough, you can compost small amounts of these if they are mixed in well.

CONTINUOUS COMPOSTING VS. BATCH COMPOSTING

One decision you need to make is whether you'll do continuous composting or batch composting. Most backyard composters do continuous composting, in which they add materials little by little, simply because they don't have a lot of compostable material on hand at one time. If you compost this way, it will be harder to heat up your pile, and your compost will process more slowly. Batch composting involves putting the necessary materials together all at once and adding proper moisture and aeration. If done right, this is the best way to achieve a hot compost pile. Batch composting is easier if you have a large quantity of materials available, or if you're using a turning unit (explained below). Sometimes it makes sense to store greens and browns separately until you have enough to make a full batch all at once.

SETTING UP YOUR COMPOST SYSTEM

Depending on your space, budget, and amount of time you want to spend, there are many ways to manage your compost system.

Probably the simplest and most traditional way is to have an open pile. In order for it to work efficiently, it needs to be at least 3 feet (91 cm) high, 3 feet (91 cm) wide, and 3 feet (91 cm) deep. Bigger is better, to a point: bigger piles will get hotter, but the maximum should be 5 feet (1.5 meters) by 5 feet (1.5 m)

A very simple composter can be made from a single 10-foot (3 m) piece of chicken wire or wire mesh formed into a circle and placed directly on the ground.

by 5 feet (1.5 m). Air naturally penetrates 18 to 24 inches (46 to 61 cm) into a pile from the edges, and piles that are too big can keep air out and too much water in. Big piles can also be too hard to turn.

HANDS-OFF COMPOSTING

If turning and checking a compost pile seems like too much fuss, you can always compost the anaerobic way: just dump it and leave it. Here are some ideas:

- To compost anaerobically in a pile, add water until it's at least 70 percent moisture. You don't need to turn it, but keep it covered. (Prepare for some unpleasant odors.)
- To make garbage bag compost, combine equal parts kitchen scraps, soil or compost, and newspaper. Wet it, seal it in the bag, and after several months you'll have compost. (Hold your nose when opening the bag.)
- To make submersion compost, put your ingredients in a large container, fill it with water, and allow the material to break down.
- For bucket compost, cut off the bottom of a 5-gallon (20 liters) bucket, bury it a few inches in the soil, fill it with waste, cover it with a tight lid, and forget about it for a year.
- Finally, a good way to prepare future garden beds is to dig a trench or pit and bury food scraps under at least 8 inches (20 cm) of soil.

Start the pile on bare earth to allow worms and other organisms to aerate the compost. Choose a spot that is away from trees or fast-growing vines, and remove any weeds or seeds from the area. Lay a few inches of twigs or straw at the bottom to aid drainage and help aerate the pile. Then add compost materials in layers, alternating greens and browns, 2 to 4 inches (5 to 10 cm) of greens and 5 to 7 inches (13 to 18 cm) of browns, in a kind of compost lasagna. Covering the pile will keep it moist, but not too wet, and will keep it warm in cold weather. An old piece of carpet works well for these purposes, but you can also use a tarp, wood, or plastic sheeting.

Locate your pile in a level area with good drainage, preferably not directly under a tree because tree roots can grow into the pile. If it's an open pile, it should be exposed to rain but not under a downspout. Avoid locations with too much direct sunlight (more than half a day) or too much wind, which can dry or cool the pile. Choose a location that is convenient and close to a water source but not directly against wooden buildings or fences. It is preferable to have extra room for storage of organic wastes. If you need to camouflage your compost pile, you can surround it with tall flowers or plants or use a vine trellis.

Open piles are fine for yard waste, but if you're putting in kitchen scraps, you could be inviting raccoons and other pests. If you want to compost kitchen scraps, it's best to use a closed container.

COMPOSTING UNITS YOU CAN BUILD OR BUY

The simplest type of compost container that you can make yourself is a holding unit made of a single piece of chicken wire or

Worms tend to live and feed a few inches (cm) beneath the top layer of a compost pile.

hardware cloth that is 10 feet (3 m) long and 3 feet (91 cm) wide. When formed into a circle and secured with metal ties, this single piece of wire mesh will create a 3-foot (91 cm) diameter, 3-foot (91 cm) high holding unit. This kind of composter has the advantage of being portable, and it can be lifted up to access the finished compost at the bottom. It can also be secured to the ground using 4 or 5-foot (1.2 or 1.5 m) wooden or metal stakes.

A simple square unit can be made of a 13-foot (4 m) length of inexpensive, 3-foot-high (91 cm) snow fencing and four wooden or metal posts 4 to 5 feet (1.2 to 1.5 m) tall. Similar units can be made of old wooden pallets and wire, or pieces of scrap wood and wire mesh. The best wood is cedar. Pine lasts a few years and then needs to be replaced. (Don't use pressure-treated lumber or lumber treated with creosote.) Covered with a wooden pallet or a piece of carpet, these units offer some security from animal pests and allow you to compost some food scraps at the center of the pile.

For a more permanent appearance, you can make a three-sided compost bin out of cinder blocks (or bricks or stones) stabilized by posts driven into the ground. A three-sided unit with a removable door makes it easy to turn the materials and remove the finished compost.

Another simple composter you can make yourself involves using a heavy-duty garbage can with a tight-fitting lid. Drill ½-inch (1 cm) holes in rows at 6-inch (15 cm) intervals around the can. You can stir the contents with a pitchfork, or lay the can on its side and roll it. Bolting a length of cedar lumber to the inside wall of the garbage can will help turn the contents as you roll the bin.

A three-bin turning unit can allow you to compost a large amount of yard waste—and some kitchen scraps—on a regular schedule. These units can be made of wood or wire mesh or both, and they generally have hinged lids. High-carbon and high-nitrogen materials are placed in the first bin and moistened. The pile then heats up. After the heat decreases, the pile is turned into the next bin along with more high-nitrogen material and water to encourage heating. In the meantime, a new pile is started in the original bin. After the material in the second bin heats up and cools down again, it is turned into the third bin. At the same time, the new material in the first bin is turned into the second bin. After two weeks in the third bin, the compost should be ready.

There are many types of compost bins, or holding units, that you can buy. These inexpensive units are generally enclosed on the sides and top and open on the bottom so that the compost comes in contact with the ground. These are good for residential areas; they are relatively small and are enclosed to discourage pests. However, because it is difficult to turn the compost, it can take anywhere from six months to two years to produce finished compost. Finished compost tends to settle toward the bottom; some units have small doors at the bottom for removing the finished compost. Some people find it convenient to have several holding bins: one for fresh materials, one for maturing materials, and a third for finished compost. Moving material from one unit to another allows you to mix and aerate the material more completely.

You can buy a freestanding turning unit that can be rolled or rotated to mix and aerate the contents with little effort. These are typically more expensive but offer several advantages. When turned regularly, they achieve higher temperatures and produce compost faster. In addition, they are usually well-sealed and elevated off the ground, making it hard for rodents to get in but making it easier to turn. Some units are insulated to increase temperatures, others have internal paddles for mixing, and some have two compartments for materials at different stages.

CHAPTER FOUR

KEEPING THINGS COOKING

If you set up your composting system correctly, compost will happen all by itself. But there are a few things you should know to avoid problems and keep things running well.

PREPARATION AND STORAGE

If you are collecting materials prior to composting (for example, for batch composting), be aware that high-nitrogen materials can smell if they are kept unmixed for too long with browns. Kitchen scraps should be kept in a closed container in preparation for composting to keep out animals and other pests.

Certain items need a little attention to compost smoothly. For example, citrus rinds, which break down more slowly, need to be chopped up and mixed well into the pile. You should also break up the skins of any root vegetables, like carrots or potatoes, or else they may grow in a slow compost pile. Fresh grass clippings are a great source of nitrogen, but too much at once can compact the compost and produce foul odors. Grass should be mixed

Eggshells are great for compost, but they should be crushed. Citrus peels should be cut up as small as possible because they are somewhat slow to break down.

well with a dry carbon source such as shredded dead leaves or cardboard. Paper should be shredded and mixed in thinly, and cardboard should be shredded or soaked first. Soaking is a great way to prepare many materials. Weeds with seeds or the roots of weeds can be neutralized by soaking them in water for a few weeks. If you have a chipper, thick stems and woody waste are no problem at all.

Another solution for thick, woody stems; evergreen leaves; and items like Brussels sprout stalks is to put them in a separate, slow-composting pile that may take a few years to break down. After that, the material can be added to the regular pile. Some people always keep a separate "filling" pile to collect and prepare materials before "cooking" them.

PICKLE YOUR COMPOST!

Bokashi is a Japanese technique for fermenting kitchen waste. It is an anaerobic process that uses wheat bran, molasses, and certain specially selected microorganisms, including bacilli and yeast, to pickle the waste. One advantage of bokashi is that it can process meat or fish. After a few weeks in a bokashi bucket, the waste is buried in the ground, where soil microbes finish the process of breaking it down. During the process, something called "bokashi tea" is produced. If you dilute it, you can use it to water your plants.

A mix of microorganisms is added to compost in the Japanese bokashi method, which can also handle meat and fish.

GETTING THE PILE FIRED UP

If your compost is in contact with the ground, you have every-thing you need to make compost: microbes and worms will find the material without your help. However, if you are impa-tient to get a new pile going, you can use a compost starter or activator, which can be purchased online or at a garden store. The compost activator jump-starts the decomposition process through a combination of pH balances, energy sources, and decay-causing microorganisms. Some also contain enzymes, hormones, or other additives. There are also special combina-tions of ingredients for breaking down specific materials such as wood chips and pine needles.

Some people get their piles going by adding one of the follow-ing nitrogen-rich sources that can be found around the house: blood meal, poultry, rabbit and horse manure, rabbit food, dry dog food, or bone meal. But the best activator is compost from a previous pile or rich organic soil.

To get your pile going quickly, it's best to use a mix of differ-ent materials. This will help you get the C:N ratio right and keep moisture at the right level.

MAINTAINING YOUR SYSTEM

Pests can be a problem when you compost food scraps, but there are ways to keep them away. The most important rule is not to compost meat, chicken, fish, oils, or dairy. Eggshells can pose a problem as well. When you do add food scraps, surround them with yard waste, sawdust, wood chips, or soil. Try not to leave any food exposed.

When purchasing a composter, one consideration is how easy it will be to mix the materials.

If animals are still doing midnight snack runs to your compost, you may have to take further action. First, be sure the lid fits tightly. Next, if your bin has vents, you can cover them with ½-inch (1 cm) hardware cloth or welded wire, wrap your entire bin in ½- or ¼-inch (1 or .64 cm) wire mesh, or line your bin with the mesh. Finally, if critters are burrowing from below, you may need to put your bin atop a bed of gravel or a wooden pallet wrapped in galvanized wire mesh. If all else fails, limit your outdoor compost to yard waste and compost your food scraps indoors using worms.

Four factors to monitor during aerobic composting are oxygen, warmth, moisture, and odors. You can ensure there is enough oxygen by frequently turning your pile. Another method is to add a ventilating stack before adding materials: a perforated pipe, a cylinder of wire mesh, or even a bunch of twigs tied together. Another way to improve aeration is to place the unit on a wooden pallet.

To keep the pile warm, make sure it is big enough. To keep warmth in, insulate the top with an old piece of carpet, old clothes, or a plastic bag stuffed with balled-up newspaper.

Moisture levels should be between 40 and 60 percent. If there is too little moisture, decomposition will virtually stop. If there is too much moisture, it will fill all the spaces between the particles of compost and limit access to oxygen. This leads to anaerobic conditions, which can cause foul smells. As compost decomposes, it gradually dries out. So either high-moisture wastes or more water will need to be added. When adding water, try to use rainwater, as municipal water has been treated with chemicals that suppress bacteria. The rule of thumb is that compost should be as wet as a wrung-out sponge. If you grab a handful of compost from the middle of the pile and give a squeeze, you should get no more than a drop or two of water.

Finally, a rotten-egg smell indicates anaerobic conditions, which can be managed by turning or by adding dry browns to a pile that is too wet. Too much high-nitrogen material can cause an ammonia smell, which can also be eliminated by careful blending with high-carbon materials.

CHAPTER FIVE

INDOOR COMPOSTING: CREATING YOUR OWN LITTLE ECOSYSTEM

Composting outdoors is ideal. Natural materials break down and become part of nature once again. But what about people who don't have the space? Luckily, even people who don't have a single square foot of land can let their kitchen scraps decompose naturally. They can produce compost for their houseplants or a lucky neighbor's garden through a process called vermicomposting, or composting with worms.

LET THE WORMS DO THE WORK

Of course, earthworms, or *Lumbricus terrestris*, are an essential part of any healthy outdoor composting system. They break down plant wastes both by consuming them directly and by encouraging the growth of microbes. After worms feed on decaying plant matter, they excrete worm castings, which contain smaller particles of organic matter that have been chemically transformed. Worms also feed on soil microorganisms, including fungi, protozoa, amoebae, bacteria, and nematodes. The mucus

The worms used most commonly for indoor vermicomposting are red wigglers. They are smaller than earthworms but grow and reproduce more rapidly.

in the worm's intestine is a good environment for the growth of microbes that help the worm digest complex organic compounds. Some of the worm's mucus is excreted with the castings and continues to stimulate the growth of microbes in the soil, which encourages the decomposition of organic matter. Worms also burrow holes through the compost, which helps in aeration.

When nutrients—such as nitrate, ammonium, potassium, phosphorus, calcium, and magnesium—pass through the gut of a worm, they become more usable by plants. Plants grow faster in soils with worms because of these chemical changes, along with biological and physical changes in the organic matter. In addition to being high in minerals, vermicompost improves soil structure, aeration, porosity, drainage, and moisture-holding capacity.

A downside is that vermicompost tends to have a slightly high pH and is low in magnesium. Therefore, it should be acidified (for example, by mixing it with peat) before being used, and magnesium should be added. Another consideration is that since vermicomposting does not achieve thermophilic conditions, insect eggs and pathogens will not be killed.

The worms most commonly used for indoor vermicomposting are *Eisenia fetida*, commonly known as red wigglers. (They are also known as red worms or brandling worms.) These are smaller than earthworms—usually about 3 inches (7.6 cm) long—and

Add eggshells, soil, or sand to a worm bin because worms need something gritty to help them grind up the food.

tend to live and feed in the upper organic or litter layer of soil in nature. They are ideal for composting because they thrive in habitats that are high in organic matter, they can tolerate a wide range of temperatures and moisture conditions, and they tolerate being handled. They also grow and reproduce very rapidly.

Unlike earthworms, red wigglers are able to digest cellulose, which makes them very good for breaking down kitchen scraps. They eat a lot—more than half their body mass every day. They also burrow down and eat soil that is rich in anaerobic bacteria (which could otherwise become smelly) and excrete castings with helpful aerobic bacteria. Another good worm for vermicomposting is the manure worm, or *Lumbricus rubellus*.

FINDING A HOME FOR YOUR WORMS

To compost with worms, you will need a container with 1 square foot (0.09 square meter) of surface area for every pound of organic waste that you produce each week. So a 2-foot by 2-foot (0.6 m by 0.6 m) bin could handle 4 pounds (1.8 kg) of waste per week. Figure on about 1 pound (0.45 kg) of worms for each pound of garbage you produce (though some say 2 pounds [0.9 kg] of worms for every pound of garbage). You can start out small because after a few months, the worm population will grow to fit the space. These days it's easy to find vermicomposting worms for sale by weight on the Internet. Just search for "red wigglers." (Note that suppliers won't ship them in really cold weather.)

Worm bins can be made out of plastic, styrofoam, wood, or metal (although wood can rot and metal can rust). It's easy to find plans on the Internet for making worm bins out of plastic tubs. Most worm bins have aeration vents and a drainage valve

TEA TIME!

One side benefit of composting is the ability to brew compost tea. Compost tea is a liquid fertilizer that you make from your compost and then spray on your plants.

Compost tea has beneficial microbes that help your plants and improve your soil, and it suppresses diseases. While there are many recipes for compost tea, this is the basic procedure: soak some compost in water for about two days, along with kelp or molasses to feed the microorganisms. While the compost is soaking, use an aquarium pump to aerate the solution. (You want aerobic, not anaerobic, bacteria.)

You can spray the finished solution on plant leaves, use it as a root-dip for seedlings, or soak it right into the soil.

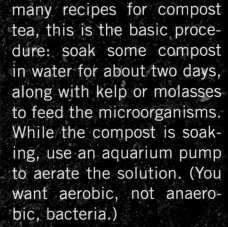

To make compost tea, steep a bag of compost in a bucket of water for a day or two. During this time, aerate the tea to encourage aerobic microbes.

for the "compost tea" that collects in the bottom, which is great for watering plants.

There are also many types of vermicomposting systems you can buy. These days, "upward migration" worm composting systems are popular. These composters have a base tray with a spigot to collect compost tea, and then three to five stacking trays on top of that. Worms, bedding, and food are put in the first of the stacking trays. When that is full, food is put into the next tray up. The worms then migrate upward through the small holes in the bottom of the tray to eat the new food scraps above, leaving finished compost below. As the worms migrate upward, you can harvest the vermicompost in the lower trays, empty them, and then have the trays ready to be added to the top.

PUTTING THEM TO BED

To prepare a worm bin, start with a good layer of bedding. You can use shredded leaves, newspaper, or cardboard soaked in water and wrung out—about as wet as a wrung-out sponge. Some bin manufacturers recommend coir, or coconut fiber. On top of that add soil, sand, ground eggshells, or sawdust because worms need something gritty to grind up their food. Always tuck the worms into their bedding along with the food scraps. One way to get them acclimated is to leave the top of the bin off with a light shining over it. They will burrow down because they hate the light. Keep your bin where it won't get too hot or too cold. Worms like temperatures between 55° and 77° F (13° and 25° C), kind of like people.

After about a week it's time to give the worms more to eat—but not more than they can handle, or it will start to stink. If possible, chop everything up into small pieces. Worms work fast; they can turn your garbage into compost in two to three months. Once the worm castings are brown and crumbly and smell like the forest floor, they're ready to be harvested. If you have an upward migration system, harvesting is simple: just remove the bottom tray. But if you just have a single bin, you have to be a little clever. Move the worm castings to one side. Then separate out any partially decomposed food and put it in the middle, along with fresh scraps. Put the lid back on and wait two weeks. The worms should all be in the food and out of the old castings. Once you remove the castings, put in new bedding and start the cycle all over again.

CHAPTER SIX

COMPOSTING FOR A CROWD

These days, composting isn't just for backyard heaps and basement worm bins. Over the last thirty years, there has been a sharp increase in the number of industrial compost facilities, both municipal and commercial. These "factory" sites process large amounts of organic waste, turning it into usable compost that is given to local residents or sold. In the beginning, it was

The city of Seattle began requiring composting of food scraps in 2009. Here, covers are placed atop piles of composting materials.

mostly leaves that were composted on this scale. But in recent years, yard trimmings, food scraps, and soiled paper have been entering the compost stream, freeing up space in landfills, where they would only produce potentially harmful methane gas. As more and more cities start requiring composting, these industrial compost facilities will become more common.

COMPOST FACTORIES

When composting on a large scale, the first problem is collection and separation. While some programs require separation of organic materials at the source, others separate organic materials from other kinds of solid waste at processing centers.

These facilities put the waste through a series of separation processes. First, it goes through a screen or trammel, which separates waste by size of particle. Then human workers do manual separation. Magnetic separation removes some metals, and eddy current separation removes aluminum, copper, and brass (aluminum cans literally jump off the conveyor belt!). Air classification sucks up lighter materials on a column of air, and wet separation uses water to separate lighter organic particles from heavier glass and metal. Finally, ballistic separation uses a spinning drum or cone to bounce harder materials, like small pieces of metal or glass, away from the compost.

Once the nonorganic materials have been separated out, the remaining material must be processed further to reduce particle size because large pieces will take longer to break down. Several devices are used for this purpose: hammermills, which consist of sets of swinging steel hammers; shear shredders, which consist of sets of rotating knives; and rotating drums. Once the particle size has been reduced, the material is mixed with water prior to microbial decomposition. If the feedstock had a large proportion of paper and therefore a high C:N ratio, nitrogen-rich materials such as sewage sludge might be added.

Industrial composting operations use a number of setups for curing compost. A very common system is known as the windrow, a long, haystack-like pile that can be 6 to 8 feet (1.8 to 2.4 m) high, 10 to 15 feet (3 to 4.6 m) across, and as much as 300 feet (91 m) long. Windrows are regularly turned using heavy equipment such as a front-end loader, a dump truck, or a specialized machine. While materials can be gradually added, windrows are usually managed as a single batch.

A worker checks the temperature of a windrow at an industrial composting facility. The ideal temperature is between 140° and 160° F (60° and 71° C).

Another system is the static pile, which is set up like a windrow but not turned. Air circulates largely through the process of convection: heat rises from the top, and cool air enters from the sides. Some static piles have forced air vents in them to aerate the compost. Otherwise, more browns—like cardboard or leaves—are mixed in to maintain a porous structure.

There are also vertical reactors that look like silos and horizontal reactors that look like long horizontal tubes. Both take in waste at one end and put out compost at the other.

Whatever the method, chances are that more American cities will soon be joining the more than ninety that currently offer curbside compost pickup. Not only is it good for the environment, but it also saves on landfill costs. Today, between composting and recycling, San Francisco diverts 80 percent of its waste from landfills, according to EMagazine.com. When Portland, Oregon, started its composting program, it cut back garbage collection to every other week.

COMMUNAL COMPOSTING

In cities around the country, even apartment dwellers have been able to get into the composting act. Greenmarkets and community gardens have become drop-off points for food waste, keeping it out of the waste stream. According to GrowNYC.org, New York residents have been dropping off food scraps at greenmarkets around the city, totaling over 1,000,000 pounds (453,592 kg) of composted waste since the program began in 2011.

In major cities, a new sort of business has emerged. Food waste pickup services cater to the restaurant and food service industry, whose trash can be as high as 85 percent compostable organic

FROM GARBAGE TO GARDEN PLOT

Members of the Earth Service Corps at Bainbridge High School in Kitsap, Washington, were determined to reduce their school's trash by 50 percent through recycling, reusing, and composting, according to an article in the *Kitsap Sun*.

Their solution for dealing with food scraps? A fully automated composter that can handle up to 500 pounds (227 kg) of food waste per day. It looks like a gigantic Dumpster with a greenhouse on top, and it has a 12-foot (3.7 m) auger to mix the material and a water sprayer to keep it wet. A biofilter uses bacteria to consume odors.

All they needed was $60,000! So they applied for grant after grant and made it happen. Now they are producing compost for the school's garden beds that will one day supply the school's cafeteria with fresh vegetables.

One of their biggest challenges was getting students to sort their waste. The solution was to give out incentives. Members of the corps rewarded students who put their waste in the right places with raffle tickets for prize giveaways.

waste. Most of the material is turned into compost. However, some is turned into energy through incineration or anaerobic decomposition, which creates methane gas that is captured and used. In Philadelphia, Pennsylvania, the Pedal Co-op picks up compostable food scraps and delivers them—by bicycle—to a composting site on an empty lot downtown known as the Dirt Factory. In Plainfield, New Jersey, Green Waste Technologies picks up residential food waste with a team of horses and a wagon! (The horse manure is captured in a diaper and broken down by fly larvae.)

Elsewhere, composting programs in community gardens have begun taking food scraps and turning them into compost right on-site. There's even a machine that businesses can buy called a Food Cycler, which reduces food waste by up to 93 percent in just twenty-four hours, turning it into usable compost, compost starter, or biofuel.

COMPOSTING AT SCHOOL

Composting organic waste at school is becoming a more common practice. According to an article in the *Star Tribune* of

A member of a compost group drops off food waste at a community garden in Brooklyn, New York.

Minnesota, about 80 percent of a school's waste comes from its cafeteria, and about three-quarters of that is organic waste.

When schools decide to start composting on a large scale, they often have to perform a waste audit first. This means they need to figure out how much waste they produce and what kind. They may need to obtain start-up money to get the program going, usually by applying for a grant. Once the program is in place, students often serve as "zero waste monitors," advising other students on how to dispose of waste materials. Some schools bring food waste to community garden programs. Others set up their own worm bins.

According to Earth911.com, five New York parents decided to set up a pilot composting program in eight schools, including replacing plastic trays with compostable ones. They wound up reducing the schools' cafeteria waste by 85 percent, saving 450 pounds (204 kg) of food waste from landfills daily, and saving an estimated $3,000 in garbage bags and $3,700 in disposal fees yearly.

Around the country, parents and teachers are becoming interested in setting up composting programs at schools as a way of teaching social responsibility and a little bit of science.

Whether it's at school, at the office, at an industrial composting facility, or just in a pile in the backyard, an increasing number of people all over the country are managing the breakdown of their organic waste. They are keeping it out of landfills and turning it into rich compost to nourish plants organically. When you compost, you break down yesterday's waste to build up tomorrow's soil.

GLOSSARY

ACTINOMYCETES Bacteria that resemble fungi and help degrade tough debris in compost.

AERATION The process of supplying with air or exposing to the circulation of air. In composting, this is usually done by turning or ventilating the compost pile.

AEROBIC Occurring in the presence of oxygen.

ANAEROBIC Occurring in the absence of oxygen.

BACTERIA Microscopic single-celled organisms that can be either aerobic or anaerobic.

CELLULOSE The main substance in the cell walls of plants, used in making paper and artificial fibers.

CURING The last stage of composting that occurs after much of the material has been decomposed. The process provides for additional stabilization and reduction of pathogens and allows further decomposition.

DECOMPOSITION The breakdown of organic matter through microbial action.

FEEDSTOCK The raw material used for a chemical or biological process.

FUNGI Plants that lack chlorophyll and feed on decaying organic matter; they include molds, rusts, and mushrooms.

HUMUS The organic component of soil formed by the decomposition of animal or vegetable matter.

MACROORGANISM A living organism visible to the naked eye.

MESOPHILIC Growing or thriving in moderate temperatures, typically between 70° and 90° F (about 21° and 32° C).

METHANE A greenhouse gas created naturally in marshes and bogs, as well as landfills.

MICROBE A tiny living organism that can be seen only with the aid of a microscope; a microorganism.

MUNICIPAL SOLID WASTE Garbage; waste generated in households, businesses, and institutions.

PATHOGEN An organism, such as a virus, bacterium, fungus, or protozoan, that is capable of producing an infection or disease in a susceptible host.

POROSITY The state of having pores or other small spaces that can hold a gas or liquid and allow it to pass through.

PSYCHROPHILIC Growing or thriving in cold temperatures, typically between 30° and 55° F (about -1° and 13° C).

THERMOPHILIC Growing or thriving in hot temperatures, typically between 104° and 160° F (about 40° and 71° C); heat-loving.

VOLATILE ORGANIC COMPOUND (VOC) A compound of carbon that participates in atmospheric photochemical reactions. In general, VOCs have high vapor pressure, low-to-medium water solubility, and low molecular weight.

WORM CASTINGS Worm feces, which contain organisms beneficial for plant growth.

FOR MORE INFORMATION

Canadian Gardening
Transcontinental Media, Inc.
25 Sheppard Avenue West, Suite 100
Toronto, ON M2N 6S7
Canada
(416) 733-7600
Web site: http://www.canadiangardening.com
This magazine's Web site has a number of pages about making
   compost, composting bins, worm composting, composting
   Christmas trees, and more. It also offers articles on garden-
   ing with kids.

Compost Council of Canada
16, Northumberland Street
Toronto, ON M6H 1P7
Canada
(877) 571-GROW [4769]
Web site: http://www.compost.org
The Compost Council of Canada's Web site is the central net-
   work for Canada's compost industry. It features resources,
   a newsroom, a section on how to make and use compost,
   background on composting in Canada, and more. The site
   is in English and French.

National Wildlife Federation
P.O. Box 1583

Merrifield, VA 22116-1583
(800) 822-9919
Web site: http://www.nwf.org/Eco-Schools-USA.aspx
This organization's Web site contains information on compost
    and other environmental issues. It has blogs for young
    people, news stories, and more. It shows how composting
    fits into the larger world of environmental action. It also
    offers advice for greening your school.

Rodale Institute
611 Siegfriedale Road
Kutztown, PA 19530-9320
(610) 683-1400
Web site: http://rodaleinstitute.org
The Rodale Institute is a nonprofit organization dedicated to
    research and education about organic farming. It offers a
    high school biology curriculum focusing on soil biology
    and the biosphere and a Young Scientist Program, which
    involves hands-on learning at the farm. Its Web site offers
    information about organic gardening, soil, and composting.

U.S. Composting Council
5400 Grosvenor Lane
Bethesda, MD 20814
(301) 897-2715
Web site: http://compostingcouncil.org

The U.S. Composting Council's Web site offers information for home composters, students, and teachers and those interested in industrial composting. It provides links to local composting programs, FAQs, and free worksheets and reports.

U.S. Environmental Protection Agency
Office of Resource Conservation and Recovery (5305P)
1200 Pennsylvania Avenue NW
Washington, DC 20460
(202) 272-0167
Web site: http://epa.gov/epawaste/conserve/composting
This government Web site provides information and advice on composting. It contains a special section with educational material for students of all ages. Its teen area includes games, tips, career ideas, and more. There are also resources for teachers, including information about student awards and grants.

WEB SITES

Due to the changing nature of Internet links, Rosen Publishing has developed an online list of Web sites related to the subject of this book. This site is updated regularly. Please use this link to access the list:

http://www.rosenlinks.com/UGFT/Comp

Appelhof, Mary. *Worms Eat My Garbage*. 2nd ed. Kalamazoo, MI: Flowerfield Enterprises, 2007.

Cromell, Cathy. *Composting for Dummies*. Hoboken, NJ: Wiley Publishing, 2010.

Curley, Robert. *New Thinking About Pollution* (21st Century Science). New York, NY: Britannica Educational Publishing in association with Rosen Educational Services, 2011.

Davies, Stephanie. *Composting Inside and Out: 14 Methods to Fit Your Lifestyle*. Cincinnati, OH: Betterway Home, 2011.

Hanson, Beth. *Easy Compost* (BBG Guides for a Greener Planet). Brooklyn, NY: Brooklyn Botanic Garden, 2013.

Lowenfels, Jeff, and Wayne Lewis. *Teaming with Microbes: The Organic Gardener's Guide to the Soil Food Web*. Rev ed. Portland, OR: Timber Press, 2010.

Markham, Brett L. *The Mini Farming Guide to Composting: Self-Sufficiency from Your Kitchen to Your Backyard*. New York, NY: Skyhorse Publishing, 2013.

McLaughlin, Chris. *The Complete Idiot's Guide to Composting*. New York, NY: Penguin, 2010.

Pleasant, Barbara, and Deborah L. Martin. *The Complete Compost Gardening Guide*. North Adams, MA: Storey Publishing, 2008.

Scott, Nicky. *How to Make and Use Compost: The Ultimate Guide*. Totnes, Devon, England: Green Books, 2010.

Smith, Kelly. *How to Build, Maintain, and Use a Compost System: Secrets and Techniques You Need to Know to Grow the Best Vegetables*. Ocala, FL: Atlantic Publishing, 2011.

Spiegelman, Annie. *Talking Dirt: The Dirt Diva's Down-to-Earth Guide to Organic Gardening*. New York, NY: Penguin Group, 2010.

Spilsbury, Louise. *Waste and Recycling Challenges* (Can the Earth Survive?). New York, NY: Rosen Central, 2010.

Squire, David. *The Compost Specialist*. London, England: New Holland Publishers, 2009.

Vincent, Wendy. *The Complete Guide to Working with Worms: Using the Gardener's Best Friend for Organic Gardening and Composting*. Ocala, FL: Atlantic Publishing, 2012.

Weise, Sandra. *The Best Place for Garbage: The Essential Guide to Recycling with Composting Worms*. Boulder, CO: WiR Press, 2011.

Woolnough, Mike. *Worms and Wormeries: Composting Your Kitchen Waste...and More!* Preston, England: Good Life Press, 2010.

BIBLIOGRAPHY

Ahmed-Ullah, Noreen S. "Composting at Schools: Students Get into the Act." *Chicago Tribune*, November 3, 2009. Retrieved March 15, 2013 (http://articles.chicagotribune.com).

Baurick, Tristan. "Students Take Lead in Successful Composting Initiative at Bainbridge High." *Kitsap Sun*, June 13, 2010. Retrieved March 15, 2013 (http://www.kitsapsun.com).

Belli, Brita. "Trash Lessons from the Greenest City." EMagazine.com, April 15, 2013. Retrieved April 20, 2013 (http://www.emagazine.com).

BioCycle.net. "Composting Roundup." September 2012. Retrieved April 1, 2013 (http://www.biocycle.net).

Bitti, Mary Teresa. "Growing City Composting Company Puts Brakes on Franchising After Dragons' Den Appearance." *Financial Post*, January 28, 2013. Retrieved March 15, 2013 (http://business.financialpost.com).

Caldwell, Christina. "NYC Schools Cut Food Waste by Composting." Earth911.com, July 10, 2012. Retrieved March 15, 2013 (http://earth911.com).

Christian, Sena. "Roseville Teens Compost School's Food Scraps." *Press Tribune*, March 9, 2012. Retrieved March 15, 2013 (http://www.thepresstribune.com).

Destries, Michael. "New York City to Launch Pilot Curbside Composting Program." Ecorazzi.com, February 14, 2013. March 15, 2013 (http://www.ecorazzi.com).

Ebeling, Eric. *Basic Composting: All the Skills and Tools You Need to Get Started*. Mechanicsburg, PA: Stackpole Books, 2003.

Flowerdew, Bob. *Composting*. New York, NY: Skyhorse
    Publishing, 2012.

Gonzales, Ron. "Santa Ana Teens Spearhead Composting
    Effort." *Orange County Register*, May 17, 2012. Retrieved
    March 15, 2013 (http://www.ocregister.com).

Grover, Sami. "Heating Your Shower with Compost."
    TreeHugger.com, March 8, 2011. March 15, 2013 (http://
    www.treehugger.com).

GrowNYC.org. "Food Scrap Collection Passes the One Million
    Pound Mark." January 8, 2013. Retrieved April 1, 2013
    (http://www.grownyc.org).

Ho, Solarina. "Canadian Teen Speeds Degradation Process for
    Plastic Bags." CSMonitor.com, June 18, 2008. Retrieved
    April 1, 2013 (http://www.csmonitor.com).

HowToCompost.org. "Composting: The Basics." 2010.
    Retrieved March 15, 2013 (http://howtocompost.org).

Iowa State University, Department of Agricultural and
    Biosystems Engineering. "Using Compost for a Safer
    Environment." May 1, 2003. Retrieved March 13, 2013
    (http://www.eng.iastate.edu/compost/faq.html).

Johnson, Lorraine. "The Secret to Making Good Compost."
    Canadian Gardening, 2012. Retrieved March 15, 2013
    (http://www.canadiangardening.com).

Jones, Ricky. Interview with the author. March 11, 2013.

Keim, Brandon. "Teen Decomposes Plastic Bag in Three
    Months." Wired.com, May 23, 2008. March 15, 2013
    (http://www.wired.com).

Lemagie, Sarah. "School Composting Is Growing 'Dramatically.'" *Star Tribune*, January 19, 2008. Retrieved March 15, 2013 (http://www.startribune.com).

Mother Earth News. "Compost Water Heater." July/August 1981. Retrieved March 15, 2013 (http://www.motherearthnews.com).

Navarro, Mireya. "Urban Composting: A New Can of Worms." *New York Times*, February 18, 2009. Retrieved April 1, 2013 (http://www.nytimes.com).

Parrish, Rogue. "How to Compost at Work." NationalGeographic.com, March 15, 2013. Retrieved April 1, 2013 (http://greenliving.nationalgeographic.com).

Scott, Nicky. *Composting: An Easy Household Guide.* White River Junction, VT: Chelsea Green Publishing, 2005.

Trautmann, Nancy, and Elaina Olynciw. "Cornell Composting – Compost Microorganisms." Cornell Waste Management Institute, 1996. Retrieved April 1, 2013 (http://compost .css.cornell.edu/microorg.html).

Urban Garden Center. "Guide to Small Batch Composting." 2008. March 15, 2013 (http://www.urbangardencenter .com/how-to-compost/how-to-compost.html).

U.S. Composting Council. "USCC Position Statement: Keeping Organics Out of Landfills." 2011. Retrieved March 15, 2013 (http://compostingcouncil.org).

U.S. Environmental Protection Agency. "Municipal Solid Waste." EPA.gov, November 15, 2012. Retrieved April 1, 2013 (http://www.epa.gov/epawaste/nonhaz/municipal/index.htm).

INDEX

A

actinomycetes, 14, 15, 16
activators, 35
aerobic vs. anaerobic, 13–14
aerobic compost systems, phases of, 20

B

bacteria in compost, types of, 15
batch composting, 24, 32
biofilters, 49
biofuel, 50
bokashi, 34
brandling worms, 40
bucket compost, 26
Burd, Daniel, 9

C

cellulose, 15, 41
chemical fertilizers, 6–7
C:N ratios, 17, 22, 35, 47
community gardens, 10, 50, 51
compost bin, buying a, 30–31
composter, building a, 27–30
compost factories, 45–48
composting
  communally, 48–50
  getting started, 22–31
  how it works, 13–21
  indoors, 36, 38–44
  large-scale efforts, 8–9, 45–51
  maintenance, 32–37
  overview, 4–12
  at schools, 4, 11, 49, 50–51
  at workplaces, 11, 51
compost tea, 42, 43

D

conduction, 20
continuous composting, 24
convection, 20
curing compost, 15, 20, 47

Darwin, Charles, 6
Dirt Factory, 49

E

Earth Services Corps, 49
earthworms, 38, 40, 41
Environmental Protection Agency (EPA), 8

F

fermentation, 34
Food Cycler, 50
Formation of Vegetable Mould Through the Action of Worms, The, 6
freestanding turning units, 31
fungi, 7, 9, 14, 15–16, 38

G

garbage bag compost, 26
grants, applying for, 49, 51
greenhouse gases, 5, 7
greenmarkets, 10, 48
"greens" vs. "browns," 22–23
Green Waste Technologies, 49
Growing City, 11

H

hands-off composting, 26
herbicides, 24
humus, 13

ABOUT THE AUTHOR

An avid locavore, Brian Hanson-Harding spends much of his free time learning about how his meat, vegetables, and dairy are produced. Aside from maintaining an extensive backyard organic garden, he buys grass-fed beef, lamb, and dairy directly from local farmers and visits the farms whenever possible. A high school English teacher, Hanson-Harding supervises a large and active environmental club, which runs the school's recycling program and organic garden, holds cleanups of the local watershed, and educates students about environmental issues. He maintains four composters at his home, including one tumbling composter and one upward-migration vermicomposter in his basement.

PHOTO CREDITS

Designer: Nicole Russo; Editor: Andrea Sclarow Paskoff;
Photo Researcher: Karen Huang